CHRISTMAS PRESENCE

Marion H. Youngquist

Poems from five decades

Drurys Publishing™

CHRISTMAS PRESENCE

First Printing

© 2006 by Marion H. Youngquist

All rights reserved. No part of this publication may be reproduced or transmitted in any form or by any means, electronic or mechanical, including photocopy, recording, or any information storage and retrieval system, known or unknown, without permission in writing from the publisher. Address all inquiries to Publisher.

Library of Congress Control Number: 2006931021

ISBN-13: 978-0-9770533-5-3

ISBN-10: 0-9770533-5-0

www.druryspublishing.com

KENTUCKY

Printed in the United States of America.

For the family

Ted

Eric and Barbara Youngquist
Marcia and Ed Hunter
Margaret and Steve Fleming
and especially
Mary and Al Karalis (deceased)

Because of Mary, the first Christmas poem was written

grandchildren

Kevin Mattson
Daughters—Brittany and Ashley

Kirk and Joanna Mattson
Children—Marion May and Trudie Faye

Rebecca Fleming
William Fleming

Jonathan Karalis (deceased)
Jeffrey Karalis
Melissa Karalis

TABLE OF CONTENTS

Preface	9
At the Stable	11
Mary's Chant	12
Weaving	13
Lullaby	14
Joseph	15
Strange Dreams	17
The Innkeeper Remembers	18
Did You See That Star?	20
The Shepherds	21
Invitation	22
King Herod	23
The First Wise Man	24
The Second Wise Man	25
The Third Wise Man	26
The Magi Slave	27
On Watching Simeon	28
Anna	29
Adoration	30
Worship	31
Response to Joy	32
Alpha	33
The Prodigals	34
The Travelers	35
John, Saint John	36
The Word of Truth	38
Waiting	39

Some Things Are Holy	40
The Search	41
A Loaf of Bread	42
Childhood Christmas	44
Lord, Send Your Peace	45
Hope	46
Christmas Comes	47
Keep Christmas	49
Direction	50
Longing	51
Compassion	52
Meditation	53
Winchester Cathedral	54
Christmas Light	55
Petition	57
About the Poet	58

Preface

How is Christmas celebrated? One way is with poetry—words in response to The Word.

Many of my poems focus on characters in the Christmas drama. I wrote them without any order. John Ciardi, a fine poet, commented that a poet must write a hundred poems before a good one is possible. I only hope one or two of these are worthy of the Christmas event.

Oddly, the first poem—*At the Stable*—was written in late September, 1954. We lived in Akron, Ohio where my husband Ted was Assistant Pastor at Trinity Lutheran Church. However, he had accepted a call to First Lutheran Church, Cedar Rapids, Iowa. Soon, we were to move—which seemed impossible because I was confined to bed, expecting our fourth child.

It was Sunday. Eric and Marcia were at Sunday School, while our toddler Margaret was at a neighbor's home. Overwhelmed, I wept. I thought, *If I can reach Christmas, perhaps things will work out.* I began to scribble. How would I have reacted to events in Bethlehem so long ago? *At the Stable* was written that autumn morning.

Somehow, we moved to Iowa in November. Our daughter Mary Ellen was born prematurely in February 1955. Although we weren't thinking of Christmas, it is appropriate that she was named Mary.

That Christmas, we used *At the Stable* on our card. Because friends responded, I wrote a second poem the next year. The tradition began. Not every annual poem was about

Christmas. However, this collection reflects the Christmas theme.

Friends and family have often asked for a book of my Christmas poetry. A *Thank You* to Sue Romo, Ruby Hauch, and Grace Gunnlaugsson for manuscript assistance and to Gary Drury, his staff, and Drurys Publishing for making this a reality.

—Marion H. Youngquist
Wauwatosa, WI.

At the Stable

What would you have done, if you had been there—
      Prattled about the weather,
      Taxes, the crowds in town,
      Gossiped about old Joseph man
And Mary, dressed in homespun gown?

What would you have done, if you had been there—
      Stroked the Baby's gentle cheek,
      His wispy hair and tight-clenched hand,
      Mused that birth is a miracle,
And spirit is God's gift to man?

What would you have done, if you had been there—
      Kneeled in awe-struck wonder
      Apart from gathered mob,
      Beheld afar a cross-fired star,
Convinced this child was born of God?

1955
2005

Mary's Chant

Hush, little Jesus boy,
the world sleeps—
restless with dreams
of riches and power.

Hush, little Jesus babe,
the inn guests complain—
your anguish disturbs
this black night hour.

Hush, little Jesus child,
earth will not listen—
your sighing, crying
is effort absurd.

Hush, little Jesus Son—
Who dares silence You?
Your screams pierce the quiet—
Your voice must be heard.

    1957

Weaving

Mary chose the softest wool,
Spun the strands both thick and thin
tangled threads to weave the bands
to wrap the baby Jesus in.

From her loom, the cloth emerged
with flaws of labor and design;
but His presence hallowed all—
her task illumined by the Divine.

1981

Lullaby

O, little Lord Jesus,
a pale star above
is seeking the manger
that cradles God's love;
a soft wind is bringing
the glorious strain
of angels a-winging
o'er Bethlehem's plain.

O, little Lord Jesus,
sleep peaceable now,
no robe to enfold you
no thorns press your brow;
sleep gentle, dear Jesus,
calm all unseen fears;
a small step soon leads you
to Calvary's tears.

O, little Lord Jesus,
we bow down this eve
with hearts full of joy
God's own Son to receive;
we praise you, adore you,
as our prayers ascend;
sing Christmas, sing Easter
Hosanna! Amen!

1962

Joseph

Joseph was a carpenter
with calloused hands, plane and rule—
he shaped a fine-grained plank
into a sturdy stool;
he planned, drew, and daydreamed
how his future home would be
with his betrothed nearby—
the young dark-eyed Mary;
that dream soon went awry
when with a plaintive cry,
Mary—-hesitant, ashamed—pled
a mystic tale of talking
to an angel Gabriel;
tossing in the restless night
Joseph—eyes, hot and dry—stared
up at the starry sky and thought
to end their pledge; finally
at dawn deep merciful sleep
brought a first angelic dream,
not of grapes or cows or corn
like his earlier namesake—
but of an ancient prophecy;
then Caesar's tax decree
directed him
"Take Mary to Bethlehem;"
a second dream— "Go to Egypt land—
escape King Herod's mad command;"

another dream returned the three
to Nazareth in Galilee
where patient aging Joseph
with calloused hands, plane and rule
taught his inquisitive son
how to shape a fine-grained plank
into a sturdy stool.

1984

Strange Dreams

Some nights need a special dream—
Joseph, restless and betrayed,
dreamed a dream and resolved
still to keep the peasant maid.

Another night strange sages
appeared at Joseph's door,
found a new-born sovereign—
old Joseph dreamed once more.

The three stole off to Egypt—
then a third dream came to him,
"Fear not, return in safety
to your Judea home again."

Every dark night needs a dream
and a star as constant guide;
within the Christmas moment
dreams and hope both still abide.

1983

The Innkeeper Remembers

In jest
you would suggest
I played the host
to angels, unaware? At most
those two were peasants
in debt to my benevolence.

Since the mother's time was near,
I lent a sympathetic ear—
For business' sake is my creed
(returning more than open greed)
I granted them the stable rear.

My reward?
A shepherd horde—
like raiders
or mad invaders
descended on the inn
with noisy din,
begging a fantastic claim
to worship him
of Messianic fame.
Ha! Over those who could—
or would reign?

At any rate,
my paying guests
were all upset;
I gave notice that the three
simply could not stay,
although simple Joseph
promised quick to pay;
he made the bench
so sturdy, standing there;
I soon extracted more—
promise of a pair;
(no businessman he was,
but I showed him just cause
to pay his cost—full fare).

What happened to the three?
Thank God, they live away from me.
What's a businessman to do?
Competition keeps our guest list few;
I like a clientele
more suitable, clean and—well,
more intelligent.
This Christ event
causes such
embarrassment.

1964

Did You See That Star?

Hallelujah! Did you see that Star?
Was it one—
or a myriad
of suns—
that pierced the nether gloom;
a curious brilliance
seeking a stable room?

Perhaps God flung
a diamond
against the sin-black sky—
splintered fragments
dazzling spilling down from on high.

Hallelujah! It was a sight,
spangling the velvet night;
but that star dimmed.
High and lifted up
His Light shall be great,
drawing all men unto Him.

Hallelujah! Did you see that Star?

1958

The Shepherds

Scramble, struggle through the bramble,
run and stumble to Bethel town;
clatter, rattle over cobble,
clutching close a rough wool gown;
simple, uncouth, noisome shepherds
rouse friends with exultant cry—
"Drunk!" the Innkeeper accuses—
"Drunk with joy!" bursts their reply;
quiet on the manger threshold,
filled with awe, silenced by fright—
"He's not like us," they kneel and whisper,
thrice crows the cock at morning light.

1960

Invitation

The Babe in the stable
lifts his small warm hands
stirring midnight air
to reach for a star
and without our commands
reaches out to us now
to lead us afar
and into His future.

    1988

King Herod

King Herod sits uneasy on his throne,
his fingers drumming in staccato time—
nervous tappings echo unseen fears
cross-current in his crafty evil mind.

He seesaws with the nomads' tale
of some new king; yet Caesar's throne—
his gold—his arms—appear secure.
Where still remains a realm unknown?

And Caesar's road leads all to Rome,
his ring imprints each shrewd demand,
only heaven remains aloof—
who moves its legions by command?

Who dares to challenge Caesar's reign?
A fool—or god—greater than stone?
With fingers drumming in staccato time,
King Herod sits uneasy on his throne.

1965

The First Wise Man

What could I bring
the King?
I first found the prophecy
and led the eastern band
to Judea land.
A poor scholar,
I sold all
for a single coin of gold—
a glittering disk
for the Child to adore.
He grasped it eagerly,
turned it over,
studied it soberly,
bit it—
and threw it on the floor.

    1956

The Second Wise Man

I was more wise
than rich,
which
seemed reason enough
to bring the chest
of frankincense,
used in every shrine
as offering divine;
let me assure—this
mark of holiness
gained new significance,
contrasted with the ruder smells
and gentle clinking of cowbells;
as I viewed his face,
this holy act of grace
seemed a lesser thing—
only grateful homage
due a King.

1966

The Third Wise Man

A King to hail?
How well
I know the smell
of royalty.
Fittingly,
I brought myrrh—
about my palace rooms,
my thousand wives
all bathed in its perfume.

Imagine my dismay
to find the new Prince
where the asses stay;
the stench offended—
yet, I can't forget—
that when I kneeled
in twilight dim,
I knew the royal myrrh
was not good enough
for Him.

        1959

The Magi Slave

I want to tramp the broad highway,
not thorny path or rocky road.
I long to lie in marble halls,
but offered pilgrim's thatch-straw bed.
I crave a sensual rich perfume
instead of stable cow-dung smell.
I much prefer sweet honeyed creams,
indifferent to blessed daily bread.
Child's hand, so warm,
clasps mine, so rough;
my murmurs cease—
He is enough.

1997

On Watching Simeon

There stands old man Simeon—
quite past his earlier prime,
mouthing the well-known *Nunc*—
that rhyme from ancient time.

"Lord, let me die in peace—
Thy promise now is sealed;
for I see Thy salvation
which claims the world with zeal;
a Light to those enslaved,
and David's Star revealed."

He lifts a palsied hand
in gesture slow, senile—
insists that God must bless
this unknown peasant child.

1990

Anna

Remember foolish Anna—
how little ones were kept
from her half-blind peer,
afraid of hex or spell
by one so old and queer?
With every girl, she sighed—
"Too bad, you tried;"
and shook her head at each boy—
"No, he's not Israel's joy."

All day she lingered long
to stay in the temple—
kneeling to pray,
muttering a long and tiresome prayer.
The priests wished to be rid of her
for true piety is hard to bear.

From Galilee
two finally
brought forth a son,
and Anna cried,
"The Messiah! He's the one!"
And then she died.

Remember foolish Anna?

1961

Adoration

On Christmas Day, great bells will ring.
Who dares approach our Christ-Child King?

Three magi watching yonder star,
an angel host—who wing to earth,
a donkey—tired of plodding far,
a couple—pondering a birth;
rough shepherds run from grassy fields;
an innkeeper loans a cold, rude bed
(boasts his good deed, but see he kneels);
though stumbling, falling—all are led.

Today we come to manger stall,
and find there's room for each, for all.

Dark natives chant on palm-fringed isle,
pale people pray with eastern twang,
'mid city din, a ghetto child
repeats the hymn the angels sang.

1967

Worship

A city set on a hill
cannot be hid—
Salamanca Spain
is such a place—
golden baroque chapels
of hushed grace
bid worshipers
to kneel and pray.

So it must have been
in Bethlehem
when in wonder
some knelt awhile
before the Child—
then, with hope,
went on their way.

1977

Response to Joy

What shall I sing at Christmas?
Like angel antiphon,
Glory to God on high
will be my joyful song.

What shall I see at Christmas?
A shining silver star—
a light to guide through gloom
the wisest from afar.

What shall I write of Christmas?
That God came from above,
His own to seek and save
in sacrificial love.

What shall I do at Christmas?
As shepherds old adored—
I'll kneel before the cross
and altar of the Lord

1963

Alpha

The world goes on
   its frantic way
   and celebrates
   a holiday.

But we few—
   like those
   who went
   that silent night
   to view
   the Christ event—
leave the crowded street,
and kneeling here
at chancel cross
find where
trust and wonder meet.

   1972

The Prodigals

The broken thong hangs limply
and the sandal's thrown aside;
the naked foot is bruised
with hurts we cannot hide;
for we are like the prodigal
in the desert of desires,
in the wasteland of our wants,
begging warmth from burned-out fires.

We can travel home again
to seek that special place,
where a patient father waits
and loving arms embrace,
bestowing grace and goodness
better than a diadem;
oh, the road for us—poor prodigals—
begins in Bethlehem.

          1974

The Travelers

Like those—
     strangers in the night
     too timid to stay
     where
     thick carpets
     damask walls
     invite repose,
     we turn away
     to seek a lesser place
     and find
     in dim stable gloom
     there
     is warmth
     and room.

     1975

John, Saint John

Did I hear John? Oh yes!
In spite of certain certainties—
like death, war and higher taxes—
John had a vision;
some thought him mad, some—a clown,
so they chased him from the temple
right out of town.

Down by the river he went,
baptizing like a crazy prophet sent
to preach some wild words;
He said, "Be merciful, forgive and repent—"
hard verbs for those who heard;
in deference, I listened for a day
to this holy fool;
then I went on my way.

Cut it any way you like;
I believe common greed
wins over the single good.
What happened to John?
Misunderstood, he lost his head—literally—
and is dead, quite dead.

I hear his cousin Jesus
(the latest family embarrassment)
comes now with much the same stance;
perchance, I'll hear him too—
I don't know; but this I do—
that John had a vision.

Once in awhile,
I'll stop along the riverbed
and feel again the bittersweet ecstasy
of what he said;
if only, just once, I could see
the hope and glory that he saw
and touch the Infinite
in awe—the mystery called
God.
Thus, in odd moments,
I ponder John and his vision.

1969

The Word of Truth

Jesus Christ was born in Bethlehem,
He shunned a scepter and a diadem,
God's word made flesh—
He lived grace and truth,
His message to love, not condemn.

Jesus said, "See lilies, fragrant with perfume,
They toil not, spin not, nor do they consume;
Yet, King Solomon
In rich royal robes
Can't compare with their glorious bloom.

Do not ask what you shall eat or drink or wear,
The world will seek them, yet be unaware
That God provides
For each tiny bird,
And for you, blessed by God's love and care."

Jesus Christ was born in Bethlehem,
He shunned a scepter and a diadem,
God's word made flesh—
He lived grace and truth,
His message to love, not condemn.

1999

Waiting

A star pierced the blackness
and dazzled the sky;
a song pierced the silence
as angels swept by;
a cry pierced the night hour;
small hands pierced the air,
so shepherds and sages
might find welcome there;
soon nails pierced His wide hands
and pain pierced Him then;
oh, when will His love pierce
the passions of men?

1970

Some Things Are Holy

Some things are holy,
some things are sacred—
vows at the altar,
His hallowed name said,
His book being studied,
His grace being spread;
wine in the chalice,
His wafer of bread.

His day and His Son
the world dares profane;
His Word became flesh,
His saints to sustain,
revealed through small things—
in stars magi saw,
an angel and maid,
a manger of straw.

His spirit brings light
with blessing untold;
we foolish made wise
as mercies unfold;
faith, hope, and love are
gifts to the lowly,
who honor His sacred
things that are holy.

1973

The Search

Where is the Babe of Bethlehem?
    Tourist buses in the square,
    hawkers selling olive ware,
    incense, flashbulbs mingle there.

Where is the Babe of Bethlehem?
    Ancient stones decry the sword
    as troops arm in grim discord—
    bones bleached like Herod's horde.

Where is the babe of Bethlehem?
    Found among the pilgrim throng
    whose clasped hands and hearts belong
    to His way of prayer and song.

There is the Babe of Bethlehem—
    His outstretched arms never cease,
    healing broken hearts with peace
    where faith, hope and love increase.

        1979

A Loaf of Bread

It was in another time,
she went with her brother
on an errand to the neighbor's farm;
when they started back,
they found on wagon rack—
put there by their neighbor's good wife—
newly baked bread
fresh and warm.
"It tasted so good," she said.

In remembrance of things past,
she comes on Christmas Eve
through snowy drifts and winter storm
to leave her own gift—
newly baked bread,
fresh and warm.

The Holy Feast began
in Bethlehem*
for there Christ was born
on Christmas morn—
the Bread of Life
who taught us to pray
"Give us today our daily bread."

And in His spirit
she was led
to give us a loaf of bread
for Christmas day;
in many ways
we all are fed.

1978

* Bethlehem means *house of bread.*

Childhood Christmas

Christmas meant
a fresh-cut fir,
pungent with an
evergreen scent;
shiny tin clips held
tiny white candles—
haloed light
that lent
wonderment—
a special glow
as we heard
"The Word made flesh"
and sang *Silent Night*
so long ago.

2002

Lord, Send Your Peace

Lord, send your peace among us—
not as the world would give
with arms and angry treaties,
old wounds none will forgive;
Lord, calm our fears and teach us
a Christ-like way to live.

Lord, send your peace among us—
true harmony instill;
indifference change to caring;
each heart, your spirit fill
as hands clasp one another—
a rainbow of your will.

Lord, send your peace among us—
with grieving hearts to heal;
we come as hungry children
to share your holy meal—
outstretched hands for bread and wine
in hope and grace, we kneel.

Lord, send your peace among us.

1995

Hope

Swiftly fly the years
of war-weary woe
and hunger for peace,
oh, let it be so;
may hearts be renewed
as Yuletide now brings
the old story retold
of swift angel wings,
starlight and shepherds,
a Babe, manger born;
hope springs eternal
on each Christmas morn.

1996

Christmas Comes

Christmas comes amid the glitter
Of our earthly holiday,
Holly wreaths and silver baubles
Fade at His nativity,
So God's spirit speaks assurance—
Christmas comes—a holy day.

Now we run like simple shepherds
With their flocks beneath the sky;
Leaving work to seek the Savior
When they hear the angel cry;
And we, too, may run and stumble;
Yet, we find Him if we try.

Now we sing with joyful voices
Words of the angelic hymn,
Bringing hope throughout the ages,
Peace on earth, goodwill to men;
Sing with joy and deep emotion;
Sing good news of Bethlehem.

Now we join in adoration
Magi from their pilgrim way;
Seeking with anticipation
King and crown on stable hay;
Come and honor, come and worship
Love expressed this festive day.

Christmas comes—with Light still shining
Brighter than displays can lend;
Trees and candles are small symbols
That the world can comprehend;
Christmas comes in old and new ways—
Wondrous Gift whom God did send.

1968

Keep Christmas

Keep Christmas—hold it tight
against the terrors of the night,
that when—
> Belief wavers, Faith can reign;
> Dreams fade, Hope can remain;
> Apathy conquers, Love can regain;

now with the rising star of morn
comes One—and Life is reborn!

1980

Direction

How far is it to Bethlehem?
    Farther than we know—
    the way is hard and thorns abound
    each careful step, more slow.

How close are we to Bethlehem?
    It isn't very far—
    be still and hear the chiming bells—
    look up and see the Star.

        2001

Longing

Wherever we may wander
or find new roads to roam,
at Christmas we seek refuge
and Bethlehem is home—
the heart's most tender haven
where tears can finally cease—
Hope carved upon its lintel
Love on its mantelpiece.

    1986

Compassion

Who helped those two
along the Judean way—
    bread, so they were fed
    wine, full-bodied red;
    sweet new-mown hay
    for a baby born
    on a star-bright morn?

Now, who helps the unknown
poor who need encouragement—
    more chiles or some clay
    to make their wares
    to sell each day?
    From open hands who lent,
    springs new life, now evident.

        2003

Meditation

Dear Lord, my heart is steadfast—
O keep me faithful forever,
Each day I sing a new song
With joy—my soul's endeavor.
At dawn I wake with longing
To play on harp and lyre string,
Giving thanks among your people;
May nations pray, praise and sing.
Your love shines farther than stars;
Your glory each day we laud;
Your faithfulness larger than clouds—
Exalt our eternal God.

2000

(Based on Psalm 57:7-11)

Winchester Cathedral

Above the dark wood choir stalls
griffins, elves and lions abound
carved by creative artisans;
their joy shaped this hallowed place
of vaulted heights and Gothic space;
on faithful watch aged saints before
wore smooth the stones on ancient floor—
now they sleep within the sacred walls.

At Evensong the great organ
resounds with a Bach chorale;
at stately pace red-robed choirs
and pious clergy process the aisle;
on russet velvet kneelers,
the contrite pilgrims pray—
each penitent's hopeful face
touched by transcendence,
blessed by grace.

2004

Christmas Light

In 1932, we celebrated
a bleak Christmas;
my Christmas stocking held
a juicy orange and
a ten-cent box of crayons;
our parents kept their tradition
of a fresh fir tree
with small white candles
in shiny tin holders,
casting a special glow
on Christmas morning.

My brother and I
were embarrassed
because the neighbors
trimmed their trees
in modern electric lights
and boxes of silver tinsel.

The next Christmas
Mama bought blue lights
and Papa strung the tree,
we *oohed* and *aahed*
and said, *It's beautiful;*
somehow, the tree
and the lights were—
ordinary.

    2006

Petition

On this blest Christmas morn,
led by star and angel song—
I steal away to stable rude
and join the kneeling throng.

I come with longing heart,
awe-struck by holy sign—
a Child who touches all with grace
and innocence Divine.

Dear Lord, grant me one gift—
inspire this heart of mine;
your Word—a feast—my daily bread,
your Life—my daily shrine.

1998

About the Poet

Marion Horn Youngquist was born and raised in Salem, Oregon. In high school she edited both the yearbook and newspaper. She repeated that experience at Midland Lutheran College, Fremont, Nebraska where she graduated. As a reporter/feature writer, she worked for The Fremont Guide and Tribune, The Oregon Statesman in Salem and the Wauwatosa Post.

She married a Lutheran pastor, Ted Youngquist. When their four children were grown, Youngquist returned to writing and editing—primarily for church publications. In the eighties, she wrote plays (won two prizes) for the Wauwatosa Village Playhouse. *Little Critters*, a published children's musical, was written with Dr. Lorraine Brugh, Valparaiso University.

A prize-winning poet, Youngquist is a member of The Academy of American Poets, The New York Dramatist Guild, Council for Wisconsin Writers, Wisconsin Fellowship of Poets and Tuesday Morning Poets—Milwaukee.

Her first novel *Procula* (about Pontius Pilate's wife) was released in 2005 and *Maple Tree Tales* (interrelated short stories) in 2006, both by Drury's Publishing.

"Our experience in New York City immediately after Nine-Eleven motivated me to write even more," Youngquist says. "I write or scribble daily. I jot down conversations that I hear and study people—in restaurants, concert halls and airports. Every stranger has a story."

She and her husband, retired, attend many classical concerts and "love to cruise". They live in Wauwatosa, WI.

www.ingramcontent.com/pod-product-compliance
Lightning Source LLC
Chambersburg PA
CBHW050919160426
43194CB00011B/2466